For You, My Husband

A 31-DAY GUIDE TO PRAYING FOR YOUR SPOUSE

Melissa Moxley

For You, My Husband: A 31-Day Guide To Praying For Your Spouse

CrossLink Publishing
www.crosslinkpublishing.com

ISBN 978-0-9852896-6-9

Library of Congress Control Number: 2014936929

To Wayne

Your encouragement and belief
in me is the reason these words are in print.
Remember that they were originally penned *for you*, **my husband**.
I love you with all my heart.

TABLE OF CONTENTS

FOREWORD

There is an old song that makes me think of you. It is called, "The Wonder of You." There is a line that says, "You take my hand and I'm a king." Though I'm not much of a king, you certainly can make me feel that I could have been one. On our bed there are eleven pillows (and I've counted them) that have to be taken off before I get to the one on which I actually sleep. A friend of mine once joked, "My gosh man, even your jeans are creased". At one glimpse, anyone can see that you feed me like a king. We live in a nicer home now, but I can remember when we lived in an 800 square foot mobile home. You made that place feel like a castle, too. You keep the checkbook balanced and make sure our children are where they are supposed to be, when they are supposed to be there. You are my wife and my queen, but more than that you are a woman of faith. It is through your faith that our home and marriage has stood the tests of the last twenty-five years. When I have become frustrated with business pursuits, as a result of market conditions or just day to day ups and downs, it is your faith that has kept us moving forward. By your faith we have a fourth child. I still remember the doctor saying, "It is a tubal pregnancy and can't be carried to term." When the doctor said, "abort," it was your faith that said, "Let us pray first" (but that's another story to be told).

You have given me so much in return for what I have to offer you. Yet you somehow still try to convince me that it is a fair exchange. You are my woman. I am blessed to call you my wife. Thank you for your faithfulness.

With love,
Your Husband

INTRODUCTION

The very fact that you have picked up this book to thumb through the pages means that you are a wife who has a deep desire to support your husband and are looking for some guidance or direction. This in itself is not unusual. God designed us, as women, to fulfill the role of support and comfort to our husbands. Genesis Chapter One tells us that we were created to be a helpmate to our spouse. It's what we often do without giving a second thought. However, this book you are holding in your hand started out very deliberately and very differently.

My husband, Wayne, and I work hard to carve out time for just the two of us. I say that because we are the parents of four children and alone time is a luxury. We were out on "date night," laughing and talking, when Wayne quickly changed topics. He began telling me about some difficulties within his business and then he looked at me and said, "You're not praying for me like you should." I didn't know exactly how to respond, so I didn't say anything for a few moments. He was not making an accusation, but more of an observation. He didn't seem to notice (or at least not enough to mention) that his khakis were freshly pressed this morning, or that last night's dessert was homemade, or that the furniture had just been polished, or how about the fact that the children were fed breakfast AND on time for school this morning (which is no small feat at our house). I was a little offended that he felt like I wasn't being a good "helpmate." After all, I have been doing a study on the woman of Proverbs 31. Apparently, it's not showing yet, and I still have a ways to go in my attempt at imitating her! After the initial sting wore off, I had to be perfectly honest … he was precisely right. My personal prayer time had been gradually drifting away from me. I was so busy doing all the things that I thought he wanted of me that I missed the thing that he most needed from me … MY PRAYERS!

I decided to commit myself to praying for my husband for the next month. Not just a general prayer for him, but to concentrate on a specific area each day for the next thirty-one days. On the first day after studying and having my prayer time, I decided to send him a short text. It went something like this: "My prayer for you today is that God give you divine wisdom. Through wisdom, leaders are raised up, long life is achieved, riches are received, and peace and happiness is provided. I love you, my husband!" He immediately responded back with love and thankfulness for the words. I told him later that night what my intentions were and he seemed genuinely appreciative that I was making this effort for him. After a couple of days, I decided to email him my words of encouragement instead of abbreviating them in text form. If he didn't receive his email by mid-morning, he would call and say, "I haven't got my devotion yet." I could tell by his reactions and my genuine enjoyment of this personal time that I was on to something. He would call to tell me how "weird" it was that the very thing I emailed him about earlier in the morning would show up in a situation later in the day that put his devotion into practice, or how a specific word was confirmed to him during that day. About the second week into this month-long journey, he asked if I was writing down these devotions because other men could benefit from their wives catching onto this. He thought that this could very well be my first published book. My heart jumped a little inside my chest, not just at the pleasure that he felt my work was good enough to be bound and printed, but because I had already had the smallest stirring within my spirit that maybe God would use these words to strengthen others.

So here you are book in hand. What is it that you are expecting from these pages? Are you looking for a quick morning devotion that can give you guidance on how to pray for your husband? Do you want an easy reference to finding scriptures on certain topics? Do you enjoy reading encouraging and sometimes humorous quotes from athletes, scholars, celebrities, pastors, philosophers, or presidents? You can get all of that from this little book, but that is not its intended use. My hope is that you use this as a tool to aid you in your personal study time. Pull out your Bible and read the scripture references that go along with each topic. Learn what God's Word has to say on the subject. Then use the prayer at the end of each lesson as a guide to praying God's blessings on your husband. They are written in the first person so you can send them directly to your spouse to let him know what you prayed for him on that particular day. I challenge you to commit yourself to this for thirty-one days. What you will find is that God will begin to not only pour these virtues into your husband, but that they will become evident in your life as well. You will feel God drawing you and your spouse closer together. Conversations will become more intimate as your husband asks you to pray about any concerns or upcoming decisions he has to make. You will see your husband striving harder to be the man God has called him to be, all because he has a wife who believes he can be. You may say I don't need to pray about this particular topic or that one because my husband already does these things. This is not meant to be an absolute, but merely a guide for you. On many of the topics in this book Wayne is a master, but it never hurts to be reminded of God's expectations of us, and Scripture never returns void (Isaiah 55:11). If your husband already possesses a certain virtue, make sure that you compliment him on it. Let your prayer for that day be one of thankfulness that God has blessed you with a husband full of wisdom, peace, patience, etc. If you find there is a particular topic that your husband struggles with, do not use this as a day to vent your frustrations or complain to him about it. If you recognize his shortcoming, you can rest assure that he knows he has it, too. The last thing your spouse needs is to get an email or text from you each day pointing out his failures. Always keep your prayers and words to him encouraging and uplifting.

In the end, do not wait to start this study. Your husband needs you to begin it. Your marriage needs you to accomplish it, and your inner spirit needs you to complete it!

Day 1
WISDOM

Proverbs 3:13-16 "Happy is the man who finds wisdom, and the man who gains understanding; for her proceeds are better than the profits of silver, and her gain than fine gold. She is more precious than rubies, and all the things you may desire cannot compare with her. Length of days is in her right hand, in her left hand riches and honor."

Proverbs 9:9-10 "Give instruction to a wise man, and he will be still wiser; teach a just man, and he will increase in learning. The fear of the Lord is the beginning of wisdom."

Proverbs 8:12-15 "I, wisdom, dwell with prudence, and find out knowledge and discretion. The fear of the Lord is to hate evil; pride and arrogance and the evil way and the perverse mouth I hate. Counsel is mine and sound wisdom; I am understanding, I have strength. By me kings reign, and rulers decree justice."

James 1:5 "If any of you lacks wisdom, let him ask God, who gives generously to all without reproach, and it will be given him."

Proverbs 12:15 "The way of a fool is right in his own eyes, but a wise man listens to advice."

Ecclesiastes 10:12 "The words of a wise man's mouth win him favor, but the lips of a fool consume him."

Quotes:

"Sir, my concern is not whether God is on our side; my greatest concern is to be on God's side, for God is always right." Abraham Lincoln

"God gave us mouths that close and ears that don't—that should tell us something." Unknown

"A wise man once said, 'An error does not become a mistake, until you refuse to correct it.'" Unknown

"Speak when you are angry and you will make the best speech you'll ever regret." Laurence J. Peter

My prayer for you today is that God give you divine wisdom. Through wisdom leaders are raised up, long life is achieved, riches are received, and peace and happiness is provided. I pray that you have the wisdom of Solomon, always possessing great understanding and realizing that all good things come from God!

Day 2

FAVOR

Proverbs 3:4 "So shall you find favor and good understanding in the sight of God and man."

Psalm 5:12 "For thou, Lord, will bless the righteous; with favor will you compass him as a shield."

Proverbs 8:35 "Whoever finds me finds life, and shall obtain favor from the Lord."

Numbers 6:24-26 "May the Lord bless you and keep you; the Lord make His face shine upon you, and be gracious to you; the Lord lift up His countenance upon you, and give you peace."

Examples in the Bible of those who found favor: Jesus, Ruth, David, Mary, and Esther

Quotes:

"The favor of God will make normal men seem like something special." Unknown

"What a great favor God does to those He places in the company of good people." St. Teresa of Avila

"Sometimes I just look up, smile and say, 'I know that was you, God. Thank you!'" Unknown

Today I pray that you find favor with God and men. Let those who meet you want to do business with you for reasons they can't even explain. I ask that God's favor rest on you like it did on David—giving prosperity and strength to stand when others do not (Psalm 30:7, "Lord, by your favor You have made my mountain stand strong," and Psalm 91:7, "A thousand may fall at your side, and ten thousand at your right hand; but it shall not come near you"). I pray that it surrounds you as a shield offering protection against anything or anyone who would do you harm (Psalm 5:12, "For You, O Lord, will bless the righteous; with favor You will surround him as with a shield"). May His favor forever be evident in your life!

Day 3
BUSINESS RELATIONSHIPS/ETHICS

Psalm 1:1 “Blessed is the man that does not take ungodly counsel.”

Amos 3:3 “Can two people walk together without agreeing on the direction?”

2 Corinthians 6:14 “Do not be unequally yoked with unbelievers. For what partnership has righteousness with lawlessness? Or what fellowship has light with darkness?”

Proverbs 19:17 “Whoever is generous to the poor lends to the Lord, and he will repay him for his deed.”

Psalm 37:21 “The wicked borrows but does not pay back, but the righteous is generous and gives.”

1 Chronicles 4:10 “Jabez called upon the God of Israel, saying, ‘Oh that you would bless me and enlarge my border, and that your hand might be with me, and that you would keep me from harm so that it might not bring me pain!’ And God granted what he asked.”

Quotes:

“Honesty is the cornerstone of character. The honest man or woman seeks not merely to avoid criminal or illegal acts, but to be scrupulously fair, upright, fearless in both action and expression. Honesty pays dividends both in dollars and in peace of mind.” B.C. Forbes

"Every young man would do well to remember that all successful business stands on the foundation of morality." Henry Ward Beecher

"The true measure of people is how they treat others who can do them absolutely no good." Ann Landers

"The world changes constantly and so does business. The only thing that remains the same is your innate abilities." Unknown

"Treat employees like partners, and they act like partners." Fred Allen

Today I pray for your business relationships. Amos 3:3 says, "Can two people walk together without agreeing on the direction?" I pray that the right people are placed in your life, people with the same ethical principles who are headed in the same "direction" as you. I ask that you will be surrounded with godly counsel in all you undertake.

Day 4
HEALTH

3 John 1:2 "I wish above all things that you prosper and be in health, even as your soul prospers."

Jeremiah 33:6 "Behold I will bring health and healing and reveal to them an abundance of prosperity and security."

Psalm 91:10 "There shall no evil befall you, neither shall any plague come nigh to your dwelling."

Psalm 139:14 "I praise you, for I am fearfully and wonderfully made. Wonderful are your works; my soul knows it very well."

Isaiah 40:29 "He gives power to the faint, and to him who has no might he increases strength."

1 Corinthians 6:19-20 "Or do you not know that your body is a temple of the Holy Spirit within you, whom you have from God? You are not your own, for you were bought with a price. So glorify God in your body."

Quotes:

"The food you eat can be either the safest and most powerful form of medicine or the slowest form of poison." Ann Wigmore

"Nothing is impossible. The word itself says I'm possible." Audrey Hepburn

"Those who think they have no time for healthy eating and exercise will sooner or later have to find time for illness." Unknown

My prayer today is that you will be in excellent health. I ask God to allow you to be cognizant of the decisions you make in regards to your health. I pray that you see the importance of making your health a top priority so we can have a long, happy, and wonderful life together!

Day 5

FATHERHOOD

Proverbs 20:7 "The righteous who walks in his integrity—blessed are his children after him!"

1 Thessalonians 2:11 "We exhorted, comforted and charged every one of you, as a father does his own children."

Psalm 103:13 "Just as a father has compassion on his children, so the Lord has compassion on those who fear him."

Psalm 103:17 "But the mercy of the Lord is from everlasting to everlasting upon them that fear him and His righteousness unto children's children."

Quotes:

"Dad—a son's first hero. A daughter's first love." Unknown

"Every father should remember that one day his son will follow his example instead of his advice." Unknown

"Love and fear. Everything a father says must inspire one or the other." Joseph Joubert

God refers to Himself as our "Heavenly Father." In Matthew 7:7-12, He tells us that all we have to do is ask of Him and He will supply all of our needs. God even compares Himself to our earthly dads. "What man is there among you who, if his son asks for bread, will give him a stone? Or if he asks for a fish, will he give him a serpent? If you then, being evil know how to give good gifts to your children, how much more will your Father who is in heaven give good things to those who ask Him!" God intends for men to be their child's first glimpse into His nature. Daddies protect, provide, and instruct. Children learn respect and reverence for God from their relationships with their earthly fathers. It is so important for a child to be able to trust in his/her daddy so he/she can grow into an adult who has faith in the Heavenly Father!

Today, I just thank the Lord for giving me a husband who is a wonderful father. I ask God to continue to show you His heart through our children. I hope you are always their comfort, love, compassion, instruction, and guidance—just as He is to His children. I know the man that you are is a blessing to our children now and will continue to be in the future (our grandchildren-Psalm 103:17).

Day 6
PATIENCE

Galatians 6:9 "Let us not be weary in doing good."

Philippians 4:6 "Don't be anxious about anything."

Romans 8:25 "If we hope for that which we see not, then do we with patience wait for it."

Galatians 5:22 "The fruit of the Spirit is love, joy, peace, PATIENCE, kindness, goodness, faithfulness and self-control."

Quotes:

"Patience, persistence and perspiration make an unbeatable combination for success." Napoleon Hill

"Patience is bitter, but its fruit is sweet." Jean Jacques Rousseau

"The key to everything is patience. You get the chicken by hatching the egg, not by smashing it." Arnold H. Glaslow

"God has perfect timing: Never early, never late. It takes a little patience and it takes a lot of faith, but it's worth the wait." Unknown

Today's prayer is that God will help you develop patience. Waiting on decisions, answers, or what-to-do next is difficult for everyone, but the person who knows how to patiently wait on the Lord's leading never messes up! I never noticed that "fruit" in Galatians 5:22 was singular. I always quoted it as "the fruits of the Spirit." An apple has several different parts (the skin, flesh, and seeds). But you still need all these parts together to make it "an apple." If we want to be a representation of God, we have to have all the "parts"—love, peace, joy, patience, kindness, etc. We can't pick and choose the parts we are good with and leave off the ones we struggle with … we have to possess them all. I ask that God grant you patience and that He give you the fortitude to graciously wait when His answers do not come in our timetable.

Day 7
PEACE

Psalm 37:11 "The meek shall inherit the earth and delight themselves in the abundance of peace."

Psalm 4:8 "In peace I will both lie down and sleep; for you alone, Lord, make me dwell in safety."

Proverbs 16:7 "When a man's ways please the Lord, He makes even his enemies to be at peace with him."

2 Thessalonians 3:16 "May the Lord of peace Himself give you peace at all times in every way. The Lord be with you."

1 Corinthians 14:33 "God is not a god of confusion, but of peace."

Isaiah 26:3 "You keep him in perfect peace whose mind is stayed on you, because he trusts in you."

Quotes:

"Peace cannot be kept by force; it can only be achieved by understanding." Albert Einstein

"Worrying does not take away tomorrow's troubles; it takes away today's peace." Unknown

"Peace. It does not mean to be in a place where there is no noise, trouble, or hard work. It means to be in the midst of those things and still be calm in your heart." Unknown

Have you ever noticed how David was constantly surrounded by people who wanted to personally do him harm or others who couldn't wait to see it happen? David's troubles were sometimes caused by his own doing (remember Bathsheba and the murder of Uriah), but many times he hadn't done anything to warrant his problems (Saul's jealousy). He would write for chapters about how everything looked bad and wonder why God allowed these people to attack him. Then over and over again he recounts how the Lord moved in each and every situation. David would see those who had come against him one by one fall by the wayside. The entire chapter of Psalm 37 is about God bringing vengeance on the wicked. Verse 7 says, "Rest in the Lord and wait patiently for him: fret not thyself because of him who prospers in the way, because of men who bring wicked devices to pass." It is easy in stressful times to look on the negative and overlook the blessings in our lives. Psalm 40:5, "Many, O Lord my God are the wonders which You have done, and Your thoughts toward us; There is none to compare with You. If I would declare and speak of them, they would be too numerous to count."

Today I pray that the Lord will give you peace of mind and spirit. I ask that you will read this and be reminded that no matter what happens in life that is out of your control, it is never out of His. I pray that you will always be a man who chooses to be a peacemaker in any situation that you are involved. I ask that God will then allow you to reap peace in the situations that are out of your hands and that you will be calmed in your spirit today remembering that He has given us more blessings than we can count!

Day 8

CONFIDENCE

Philippians 4:13 "I can do all things through Christ who gives me strength."

Hebrews 13:6 "So they may boldly say, the Lord is my helper and I will not fear what man shall do unto me."

Joshua 1:9 "Have I not commanded you? Be strong and of good courage; be not afraid, neither be dismayed: for the Lord God is with you wherever you go."

Proverbs 3:26 "For the Lord shall be your confidence and shall keep your foot from being taken."

Isaiah 41:10 "Do not fear, for I am with you; do not be dismayed for I am your God; I will strengthen and help you; I will uphold you with my righteous right hand."

Psalm 27:3 "Though an army encamp against me, my heart shall not fear; though war arise against me, yet I will be confident."

Proverbs 14:26 "In the fear of the Lord one has strong confidence, and His children will have a refuge."

Quotes:

"Aerodynamically, the bumblebee should not be able to fly; the bumblebee doesn't know that, so it goes on flying anyway." Mary Kay Ash

"God wisely designed the human body so that we can neither pat our own back nor kick ourselves too easily." Unknown

"Always hold your head up, but be careful to keep your nose at a friendly level." Max L. Forman

Today I pray that you operate in confidence. I ask the Lord to sharpen that area of your life. Unfortunately, confidence often gets lumped in with arrogance or pride, and confident people have a hard time getting respect from others. However, I found a lot of scriptures (many more than I listed above) that says we not only have the right to be confident, but it is commanded of us (Joshua 1:9). The catch is that we know where our confidence lies! The Bible is adamant about not thinking more highly of ourselves than we ought to, but that we should go about our lives unafraid of what comes next if God is our confidence. Be a man of faith. Recognize that all success is a blessing of God. Proverbs 3:6 says, "Seek His will in all you do, and He will show you which path to take." Be open to His leading and then be confident in the direction you are going!

Day 9

DISCERNMENT

1 John 4:1 “Don’t believe every spirit, but test the spirits to see whether they are from God, for many false prophets have gone into the world.”

John 7:24 “Do not judge by appearances, but judge with right judgment.”

Colossians 2:8 “See to it that no one takes you captive by philosophy and empty deceit....”

Matthew 24:24 “For false christs and false prophets will rise and perform great signs and wonders, to lead astray, if possible, even the elect.”

1 Thessalonians 5:21 “But test everything; hold fast what is good.”

1 Corinthians 12:10 “He gives one the power to perform miracles, another the ability to prophesy. He gives someone else the ability to discern whether a message is from the Spirit of God or from another spirit.”

Quotes:

“Life offers you a lot of invitations.... Be wise enough to choose which are worth attending.” Unknown

“The first point of wisdom is to discern that which is false; the second, to know that which is true.” Lucius Lactantius

Today's prayer is that you will have discernment in every area of your life. Wisdom and discernment go hand in hand and it's difficult to fully have one without the other. The Bible is emphatic that we need both to be the best we can be. It also insists that both come from God and we only receive them by praying and asking for them (James 1:5). Discernment is the ability to see the truth of a matter, even when it may be hidden. I can't think of many other things that would be more vitally important in business, church, or just life itself.

Solomon prayed for wisdom and discernment in 1 Kings 3 and God was greatly pleased with him. I guess it would be like our child coming to you and saying, "Daddy, I need your help on this. I can't do it alone and I need to learn so I can take care of myself. I want you to teach me." You would spend every dime you have and every waking moment to teach and get him the help he needs. I like to think that God looks at us asking for discernment and wisdom the same way. It shows Him that we are depending on His insight to navigate through life. I think He will do whatever it takes to make sure that we have the tools (discernment and wisdom) we need to make it happen.

I pray for God to give you the ability to "see" directly into the spirit of a matter—whether it be a situation or person that you can quickly identify what's good or what's bad. I ask that when you only get partial information, you are instinctively able to fill in the missing pieces in order to make sound decisions.

Day 10

OUR MARRIAGE

1 Corinthians 13:4-8 "Love is patient and kind; love does not envy or boast; it is not arrogant or rude. It does not insist on its own way; it is not irritable or resentful; it does not rejoice at wrongdoing, but rejoices with the truth. Love bears all things, believes all things, hopes all things, endures all things. Love never ends."

Quotes:

"A happy marriage is the union of two good forgivers." Ruth Bell Graham

"A successful marriage requires falling in love many times, always with the same person." Mignon McLaughlin

"Enjoy the little things in life … for, one day, you'll look back and realize they were the big things." Kurt Vonnegut

"There is no greater happiness for a man than approaching a door at the end of a day knowing someone on the other side of that door is waiting for the sound of his footsteps." Ronald Reagan

There are LOTS of scriptures regarding marriage. Some are directed at the husband and some are for the wife. One of my all-time favorite scriptures is 1 Corinthians 13:4-8. It is written almost poetically. Love overlooks all flaws and just sees the other person as they should be. It only believes and expects the best. It causes one to cheer at the other's accomplishments and patiently endures any failures. Love is forever….

Today I pray for our marriage. I ask God to strengthen it and allow it to grow every day. In a world where so little emphasis is placed on commitment, I pray that we have the kind of love that can only be separated by death. The health of our marriage will be evident by where it is on our list of priorities. My desire is for us to continue to pursue each other like we did when we were dating. Behind God, I want you to be my top priority and I yours. Let it be unmistakable by our daily commitments that we make time for each other. I want our marriage to be filled with laughter, kindness, passion, and happiness. I ask that God will take our individual talents, strengths, and personalities and combine them into a "one flesh" marriage that brings us and Him joy.

Day 11

ATTITUDE

Philippians 2:14 "Do all things without grumbling or complaining."

Colossians 3:17 "And whatever you do, in word or deed, do everything in the name of the Lord Jesus."

James 4:10 "Humble yourself before the Lord and He will exalt you."

Philippians 2:5 "Your attitude should be the same as that of Jesus Christ."

Philippians 1:27 "Whatever happens, conduct yourself in a manner worthy of the gospel of Christ."

Quotes:

"I have learned to accept what God allows and to change what He empowers me to change—which is usually my attitude." Unknown

"Your attitude, not your aptitude, will determine your altitude." Zig Ziglar

"A bad attitude is like a flat tire. If you don't change it, you'll never go anywhere." Unknown

Today I pray that God will help you to always have the right attitude. Even in situations where you are intentionally wronged, I hope you are always able to have an attitude like Christ's. It's funny that when I was studying on attitude, I found that Paul wrote a lot about the subject in the book of Philippians. Paul was the one in a Roman prison, yet he found it necessary to write to the church about keeping a good attitude. I guess it's been the same way since the beginning of time. People are people and they will do things sometimes that stretch the limits of your acceptance (yes, even in the church). Paul reminds us that no matter what happens, we are still expected to be Christlike in our words and actions. I pray that you will stop and check yourself before saying or doing anything that wouldn't bring Christ glory.

Day 12

HAPPINESS

Ecclesiastes 3:12-13 "I perceived that there is nothing better for them than to be joyful and to do good as long as they live; also that everyone should eat and drink and take pleasure in all his toil—this is God's gift to man."

John 14:1 "Let not your hearts bc troubled. Believe in God; believe also in me."

Psalm 37:4 "Delight thyself in the Lord and he shall give thee the desires of your heart."

Psalm 127:5 "Happy is the man that hath his quiver full of them (children)."

Proverbs 16:20 "He that handles a matter wisely shall find good; and whosoever trusts in the Lord, happy is he."

Proverbs 17:22 "A merry heart does good like a medicine, but a broken spirit dries the bones."

Quotes:

"The happiest people don't have the best of everything; they just make the best of everything they have." Unknown

"Happiness is a perfume you cannot pour on others without getting a few drops on yourself." Ralph Waldo Emerson

"Whoever is happy, will make others happy, too." Mark Twain

"Thousands of candles can be lit from a single candle, and the life of the candle will not be shortened. Happiness never decreases from being shared." Unknown

Today I pray that you are just happy. I ask that this will be a good day and good things will come your way. I hope something happens that makes you laugh out loud. Speaking of… what do you call a fat psychic?? A four chin teller! Or what do you call a man with no body and just a nose?? Nobody nose! What do you call a bear without an ear?? B. What do Eskimos get from sitting on the ice too long? Polaroids. Okay last one … what do they call pastors in Germany? German shepherds ☺ Hope this brought a smile to your face.

Day 13
FOCUS

Proverbs 3:6 "In all your ways acknowledge Him and He will make straight your paths."

Psalm 103:2-4 "Bless the Lord, oh my soul, and forget not all His benefits, who forgives all your iniquity, who heals all your diseases, who redeems your life from the pit, who crowns you with steadfast love and mercy."

Isaiah 26:3 "You will keep in perfect peace all who trust in you, all whose thoughts are fixed on you!"

Quotes:

"If you chase two rabbits, both will escape." Unknown

"You will never reach your destination if you stop and throw stones at every dog that barks." Winston Churchill

"Life is like a camera. Just focus on what's important and capture the good times, develop from the negatives, and if things don't work out, just take another shot." Unknown

Making sure we are focused on the right thing is sometimes easier said than done. We want to always do and say the right thing, but life can sometimes cloud our focus. I was reading in Matthew 14 where Jesus sent the disciples out on a boat and a terrible storm blew up. Jesus came to them walking on the water, but they were so fearful and stressed that they didn't even recognize him. Peter says, "If it is you, command me to come to you on the water." Jesus tells Peter to come and he does. Peter is defying gravity and walking on top of the water! Unfortunately, he begins to notice the boisterous wind, takes his eyes off Jesus, and starts to sink. Jesus takes his hand and helps him back into the boat. Then Jesus says, "O you of little faith, why did you doubt?"

We have to decide where our focus is going to be. I think it is a conscious choice to focus on Christ. Peter was right where Jesus told him to be and he still found himself in the middle of a storm. He was the only one willing to get out of the boat and Jesus rewarded him for it by letting him walk on water! But, then the Bible says he noticed the "boisterous wind" and began to sink. If we are where God has placed us, doing the best we can, then let's choose to focus on the good, not the boisterous wind of bad.

Today I pray for your focus to be determined and sharp. I read that the reason animal trainers, like the famous circus performer Clyde Beatty, take stools with them into a lion cage is because the lion will try to focus on all four of the stool legs at once and it will confuse and paralyze him. A divided focus always works against us. I pray that you are able to clearly see past any "storms or winds" that come your way and focus on the One who is able to calm the storm.

Day 14

CHARACTER/INTEGRITY

1 Samuel 16:7 "But the Lord said to Samuel, do not look on his appearance or on the height of his stature, because I have rejected him. For the Lord sees not as a man sees: man looks on the outward appearance, but the Lord looks on the heart."

Matthew 5:48 "You therefore must be perfect, as your heavenly Father is perfect."

Jeremiah 10:23 "I know, Oh Lord, that the way of man is not in himself, that it is not in man who walks to direct his own steps."

Titus 2:7-8 "In all things show yourself to be a pattern of good works; in doctrine showing integrity, reverence, incorruptibility. Sound speech that cannot be condemned; that one who is an opponent may be ashamed, having nothing evil to say of you."

Quotes:

"People may doubt what you say, but they will always believe what you do." Lewis Cass

"The most important persuasion tool you have in your entire arsenal is integrity." Zig Ziglar

"A person who is fundamentally honest doesn't need a code of ethics. The Ten Commandments and the Sermon on the Mount are all the ethical codes anybody needs." Harry S. Truman

My prayer today is that you will always be a man of integrity. I don't think this is a problem for you at all, but it never hurts to be reminded that you always have to guard your character. The Bible says in 1 Corinthians 15:33 that we have to be careful who we let in our inner circle or they can rub off on us. "Do not be deceived. Evil company corrupts good habits." When God judges us, He does so by looking at our integrity. David wrote in Psalm 7:8, "Judge me oh Lord, according to my righteousness and according to my integrity within me." Job 2:3 reads, "Then the Lord said to Satan, 'Have you considered My servant Job, that there is none like him on the earth, a blameless and upright man, one who fears God and shuns evil? And still he holds fast to his integrity, although you incited Me against him.'" You just can't diminish how much weight God puts on our moral actions. He has always required us to treat people kindly, fairly, and honestly. Men who practice that these days are few and far between. I am truly thankful that you are one of them.

Today I pray that you will always guard your character. I ask that people will know you are a man who does what he says he will do. You will always have a good name and your word counts for something. I pray that you are like Joseph, always taking the high road even when others do not.

Day 15
COMPROMISE

James 4:17 "Whoever knows the right thing to do and fails to do it, for him it is sin."

1 Kings 18:21 "Elijah came to all the people and said, 'How long will you go limping between two different opinions? If the Lord is God, follow Him; but if Baal, then follow him.' And the people did not answer him a word."

Revelation 14:12 "Here is a call for the endurance of the saints, those who keep the commandments of God and their faith in Jesus."

John 14:15 "If you love me, you will keep my commandments."

Daniel 3:16-18 "Shadrach, Meshach and Abednego answered and said to the King, 'Oh Nebuchadnezzar we have no need to answer you in this matter. If this be so, our God whom we serve is able to deliver us from the burning fiery furnace, and He will deliver us out of your hand, Oh King. But if not, be it known to you, Oh King, that we will not serve your gods or worship the golden image that you have set up.'"

Quotes:

"It is the weak man who urges compromise—never the strong man." Elbert Hubbard

"Compromise is but the sacrifice of one right or good in the hope of retaining another—too often ending in the loss of both." Tryon Edwards

"When you have to start compromising yourself or your morals for the people around you, it's probably time to change the people around you." Unknown

I know that there are situations where compromise is a positive thing. Marriages wouldn't last very long if one person did all the taking all the time. However, when it comes to our morals and faith, compromise becomes a very ugly thing. I was recently reading in Daniel and really realized how uncompromising he was. Daniel was just a teenager when he was stripped from his family, carried into a foreign country, forced to learn that language, and pressured to accept pagan lifestyles. They even changed his name from Daniel, which means "God is my judge," to Belteshazzar, "The god Bel is my judge." Daniel 1:8 says, "But Daniel purposed in his heart that he would not defile himself with the portion of the king's delicacies." Because Daniel accepted the king's training but not his diet, learned his language but still kept his own daily words of prayer and served the king but never acknowledged him as God, the Lord blessed Daniel. God gave Daniel favor and wisdom with those around him. He later even shut the lions' mouths when others became jealous of him (that's a good lesson in itself—God will shut the mouths of those who mean us harm when we obey Him, but that's not today's thought).

We live in a world that is pressuring us to compromise our faith in Christ and our moral codes. We are told that tolerance is the way to peace, but God is express in His Word that we are not to bend to the world's standards of religion, business, marriage, social issues, etc. Though it is not popular, there are no gray areas with God … there is black and white, right and wrong.

Today I pray that you always stand for right and that you will continue to be uncompromising in your faith. I ask that the people around you will know that you are a moral person who operates on

"The Solid Rock" and, just like Daniel, you are and will continue to be blessed because of it.

Day 16
FINANCES

Deuteronomy 8:18 "Remember the Lord your God, for it is He who gives you the ability to produce wealth."

Proverbs 13:22 "A good man leaves an inheritance to his children's children."

Proverbs 22:7 "The poor are always ruled over by the rich, so don't borrow and put yourself under their power."

Luke 12:15 "Jesus said to them, 'Watch out! Be on your guard against all kinds of greed; a man's life does not consist in the abundance of possessions.'"

Proverbs 3:9 "Honor the Lord with your wealth, with the first fruits of all your crops; then your barns will be filled to overflowing and your vats will brim over with new wine."

1 Timothy 6:10 "For the love of money is a root of all sorts of evil and some people by longing for it have wandered away from the faith and pierced themselves with many griefs."

Jeremiah 9:23-24 "This is what the Lord says: Let not the wise man boast of his wisdom or the strong man boast of his strength or the rich man boast of his riches, but let him who boasts boast about this: that he understands and knows Me, that I am the Lord, who exercises kindness, justice and righteousness on earth, for in these I delight, declares the Lord."

Quotes:

"If you want to feel rich, just count the things you have that money cannot buy." Proverb

"Never spend your money before you have it." Thomas Jefferson

"The real measure of your wealth is how much you'd be worth if you lost all your money." Unknown

"A business that makes nothing but money is a poor business." Henry Ford

It is fitting that so many verses about money are found in the book of Proverbs. God granted Solomon more wealth than any king on the earth (Proverbs 10:23). Many people believe that he is the richest man to ever live if you convert his wealth into today's dollars. At any rate, Solomon had so much silver and gold brought into Jerusalem that they were as common as rocks (2 Chronicles 1:15, 1 Kings 10:21). But, for all his wealth, Solomon says that wisdom's proceeds are "better than profits from silver and gains of fine gold" (Proverbs 3:13-14). Solomon with all his great understanding knew that men would have trouble keeping a right perspective about wealth. He teaches us to give back to God who made it possible for you to get money in the first place. He tells us to save for our children and grandchildren and not to borrow money because it will enslave us to the lender. Solomon never once says that having money is a bad thing; it's how we perceive it that can cause us problems.

Today I pray for God to continue to bless our finances. I ask that He gives you wisdom about where to invest, how to save, and what to buy. I pray that He confirms His word by making Amos 9:13 become a reality in your work/business. "Yes indeed, it won't be long now. Things are going to happen so fast your head will swim, one thing fast on the heels of the other. You won't be able to keep up. Everything will be happening at once—and everywhere you look, blessings!" (The Message). Lastly, I ask that you will always possess a giving spirit.

Day 17

ORGANIZATION

1 Corinthians 14:40 “But all things should be done decently and in order.”

Luke 14:28 “Which of you desiring to build a tower, does not first sit down and count the cost, whether he has enough to complete it?”

Proverbs 19:21 “Many are the plans in a man’s heart, but it is the Lord’s purpose that prevails.”

Proverbs 21:5 “The plans of the diligent lead to profit as surely as haste leads to poverty.”

Habakkuk 2:2 “And the Lord answered me and said, ‘Write the vision, and make it plain upon tables, that he may run that reads it.’”

Proverbs 27:23-24 “Be diligent to know the state of your flocks and attend to your herds; for riches are not forever, nor does a crown endure to all generations.”

Quotes:

“A good system shortens the road to the goal.” Orison Swett Marden

“For every minute spent organizing, an hour is earned.” Unknown

“It takes as much energy to wish as it does to plan.” Eleanor Roosevelt

"Have a time and place for everything, and do everything in its time and place, and you will not only accomplish more, but have far more leisure than those who are always hurrying." Tryon Edwards

A good example of someone being organized in the Bible is Esther (of course, it would be a woman ☺). When the king is tricked into making a decree to kill all the Jews, Esther puts a plan into action. She calls a three-day fast, plans a banquet, goes unannounced into the king's court, prepares a second banquet, and then makes her request known. I wonder what would have happened to Esther and the rest of the Jews if she had just bebopped right up to the king's throne and started asking for favors. That probably would have been the end of Esther, and King Ahasuerus would have been on the lookout for queen number three. But Esther knew the importance of taking her time, planning, and organizing herself. In the end, the Jewish nation is saved and her enemy Haman is hanged on the gallows he built for Esther's family.

Organization may sound like a silly thing to pray for, but it enables a person to work quicker and more efficiently. So, today I pray that the Lord helps you to become more organized. I ask that you have a neat and tidy desk, office, and truck, so that you are able to become more proficient in your work. As you will have more order in your files and office, I pray paperwork will become easier and projects more profitable. I hope that you have a renewed diligence and attention to detail that will make every aspect of your life more beneficial.

Day 18

HUSBAND

Ephesians 5:25 "Husbands, love your wives, as Christ loved the church and gave Himself for it."

1 Peter 3:7 "Likewise, husbands live with your wives in an understanding way, showing honor to the woman as the weaker vessel, since they are heirs with you of the grace of life, so that your prayers may not be hindered."

Proverbs 5:18-19 "Let your fountain be blessed and rejoice in the wife of your youth, a lovely deer, a graceful doe. Let her breasts fill you at all times with delight; be intoxicated always in her love."

Colossians 3:19 "Husbands, love your wives and do not be bitter toward them."

Proverbs 18:22 "He who finds a wife finds a good thing and obtains favor from the Lord."

Quotes:

"Success in marriage does not come merely through finding the right mate, but through being the right mate." Barnett R. Brickner

When Lord John Russell was asked what he would consider a proper punishment for bigamy, he answered, "Two mothers-in-law."

"Don't smother each other. No one can grow in the shade." Leo Buscaglia

"What a happy and holy fashion it is that those who love one another should rest on the same pillow." Nathaniel Hawthorne

Though the Bible doesn't talk a whole lot about Joseph, we get a good look at his character in Matthew chapters 1 and 2 and in Luke 2. Joseph was a just man who was asked to believe an incredible story (his fiancé was pregnant with the Messiah). At first, all he had was Mary's word. Joseph would have been justified by law to have her killed for her seeming betrayal, but he wasn't trying to protect his ego. He decided to quietly call off the engagement and simply try to move on. But then the angel, Gabriel, confirmed Mary's account, and Joseph immediately went into action. He took Mary as his wife and spent the next couple of years moving to different towns in order to protect her and Jesus. I believe God chose Joseph just as He did Mary to be Jesus' parent. God saw that Joseph was a man of great character. He wasn't caught up in drama; he had deep convictions, great love for Mary, and was a man's man who could offer them protection. Mary may have been able to carry out the task without Joseph, but God in His infinite wisdom knew that Mary needed Joseph to make the journey easier.

Today I pray for you as my husband and ask that we will make this journey (life) easier for each other. I pray that we are always each other's physical and emotional support and that we always remember that we were divinely placed together. I honestly don't know what I would do without you. I hope that even as I grow older, get grayer and become more wrinkled, that I will always be the one who still captures your heart, attention, and love (Proverbs 5:18-19)!

Day 19

COMMUNICATION/SPEECH

Proverbs 15:2 “The tongue of the wise makes knowledge acceptable, but the mouth of fools spouts folly.”

Proverbs 18:21 “Death and life are in the power of the tongue and those who love it will eat its fruits.”

Proverbs 12:13-14 “An evil man is ensnared by the transgression of his lips. But the righteous will escape from trouble. A man will be satisfied with good by the fruit of his words, and the deeds of a man’s hands will return to him.”

Proverbs 21:23 “He who guards his mouth and his tongue, guards his soul from troubles.”

Proverbs 11:11 “By the blessing of the upright a city is exalted, but by the mouth of the wicked it is torn down.”

James 1:19 “This you know, my beloved brethren. But everyone must be quick to hear, slow to speak and slow to anger.”

Quotes:

“When I talk to people, I spend two-thirds of the time thinking what they want to hear and one-third thinking about what I want to say.”
Abraham Lincoln

"To talk well and eloquently is a very great art, but an equally great one is to know the right moment to stop." Mozart

"Wise men talk because they have something to say; fools, because they have to say something." Plato

If there is one thing that nearly everyone has a problem with, it is controlling their tongue. The Bible speaks A LOT about listening more … talking less, but it is also adamant that as Christians, we make sure that the things we do say are uplifting and positive. I knew the scripture "death and life are in the power of the tongue," but the rest of that scripture goes, "and those who love it will eat its fruits." If we speak with kindness and caring, it will make its way back around to us; the flip side of that is if we are negative … we can expect that to come our way, too.

Remember in Numbers 13-14 when Moses sent the twelve spies to Canaan? They all agreed that it was a wonderful land, that it did indeed flow with milk and honey, and that the grape clusters were so large that it took two men to carry them! Unfortunately, that's where the agreements ended. Caleb and Joshua saw the land and said it is just like the Lord promised … Let's go take it! The other ten men saw fortified cities with strong men and giants. We look like grasshoppers compared to those guys. No way can we overthrow Canaan; we should have just died in Egypt … and for good measure, let's stone Caleb and Joshua for trying to get the rest of us killed here!

In Deuteronomy 1, we get another account of the same story. In verse 28, the Israelites say, "Where can we go up? Our brethren have discouraged our hearts, the people are greater and taller than we." Because of Israel's unbelief, they wandered in the desert for another thirty-seven years.

That was a pretty bold statement, "Our brethren have discouraged our hearts." The words of ten men cost hundreds of thousands of people (everyone over the age of twenty, except Joshua and Caleb) their lives. It also meant their last years were spent roaming around in a desert. They never got to establish homes, plant vineyards, pasture livestock, or enjoy their families in their old age. Because they listened to the negative words of a few, their lives were deeply impacted for the worst. They heeded to the words of death on the tongues of men and they ate the fruit of it.

Today I pray that your communication/speech will always be uplifting and positive. I ask that you are able to speak "life" in even the most difficult conversations. I pray that God will direct you when to speak up and when to remain quiet. And that you will eat "good fruit" from the kind words that you have sown in others.

Day 20

LEADERSHIP SKILLS

Philippians 2:3 "Do nothing from rivalry or conceit, but in humility count others more significant than yourself."

Luke 22:26-27 "But not so with you. Rather, let the greatest among you become as the youngest, and the leader as one who serves. For who is the greater, one who reclines at the table or one who serves? Is it not the one who reclines at the table? But I am among you as the One who serves."

Matthew 7:12 "So whatever you wish that others would do to you, do also to them, for this is the Law and the Prophets."

1 Timothy 4:8 "For while bodily training is of some value, godliness is of value in every way, as it holds promise for the present life and also for the life to come."

Psalm 37:5 "Commit your way to the Lord; trust in Him, and He will act."

1 Corinthians 10:33 "Just as I try to please everyone in everything I do, not seeking my own advantage, but that of many, that they may be saved."

Quotes:

"Anyone can hold the helm when the sea is calm." Publilius Syrus

"The best executive is the one who has sense enough to pick good men to do what he wants done and self-restraint enough to keep from meddling with them while they do it." Theodore Roosevelt

"Lead from the back—and let others believe they are in front." Nelson Mandela

"Alexander, Caesar, Charlemagne, and I founded empires. But on what did we rest the creations of our genius? Upon force. Jesus Christ founded his empire on love; and at this hour, millions of men would die for Him." Napoleon

The Bible is full of examples of great leaders. Jesus taught us that leaders should first be servants. Peter showed us that they bounce back even after great failure. David was not afraid to stand and fight for what was right. Joseph persevered under dire circumstances. Joshua was a man who led by example. Noah obeyed and was righteous when nobody else was. Job was counted trustworthy even by God Himself. Ruth possessed loyalty, the Widow retained a giving heart, and Esther displayed courage.

Today I pray for you as a leader. May you lead in our home, business, and church. I ask God to give you every virtue of a great leader. I pray that you are an example to those around you and are able to see others' potential and pull it out of them. True leaders are not just looking to make themselves great; they bring greatness out in others. I know that there is still a lot that you would like to accomplish, so I pray that you become all that God and I know you can be.

Day 21
MOTIVATION

1 Corinthians 15:58 "Therefore, my beloved brethren, be steadfast, immovable, always abounding in the work of the Lord, knowing that in the Lord your labor is not in vain."

Colossians 3:23 "Whatever you do, work heartily, as for the Lord and not for men."

Exodus 19:5 "Now therefore, if you will indeed obey my voice and keep my covenant, you shall be my treasured possession among all peoples, for all the earth is mine."

Ecclesiastes 9:10 "Whatever your hand finds to do, do it with all your might."

Philippians 4:13 "I can do all things through Christ who strengthens me."

Psalm 62:5 "Wait silently for God. He is my rock and my salvation, He is my defense; I shall not be moved."

Quotes:

"People often say that motivation doesn't last. Well, neither does bathing—that's why we recommend it daily." Zig Ziglar

"You can't build a reputation on what you are going to do." Henry Ford

"Only I can change my life. No one can do it for me." Carol Burnett

"You are never too old to set another goal or to dream a new dream." C.S. Lewis

Motivation is the reason we act or behave a certain way. God instructs us in scripture to always do our best and work hard. He has to be our motivation for everything we do or else we will find ourselves in a rut and unhappy with our lives. If we can't see how Christ is involved in all aspects of our lives, then our jobs become drudgery, church becomes an obligation, and relationships become meaningless. We must give everything we do our all.

Elijah was a man whose motivation was to turn Israel back to the one true God. In 1 Kings 16, the Bible tells about a man named Omri who became king. Omri was a man who did evil in the eyes of the Lord, more so than any king before him (verse 25). When he died, his son Ahab ruled in his place and the Bible says he was even worse than his father (30-33). Ahab and his father, Omri, built idols and led the Israelites to sin against God. Elijah didn't just refuse to worship Baal; he was determined to prove once and for all to Israel that the Lord was God. Elijah found himself on a mountaintop with the prophets of Baal, outnumbered 450 to one. However, he never doubted or feared what he was called to do; in fact, when Baal failed to answer his followers' prayer with fire, Elijah taunted and mocked these false prophets. Elijah tells the people, "How long will you falter between two opinions? If the Lord is God, follow Him; but if Baal, follow him." But the people didn't answer him. He couldn't get one person to speak up on behalf of God … not one. Elijah understood the meaning of motivation. His behavior and actions were that of a man dedicated to God. You know how the story ended...God immediately answered Elijah's short prayer. Motivated people capture God's attention.

Today I pray that your motivation is stronger than it has ever been. I ask that you find a renewed enthusiasm in your work, that church is an inspiration again and our family is always one of your greatest incentives. Whatever your hand finds to do, do it with everything that is inside of you! I pray that He is the drive behind all that you set out to do!

Day 22

TRUST

Psalm 9:10 "Those who know your name will trust in you, for you, Lord, have never forsaken those who seek you."

Psalm 13:5 "But I trust in your unfailing love; my heart rejoices in your salvation."

Psalm 28:7 "The Lord is my strength and my shield; my heart trusts in him and I am helped. My heart leaps for joy and I will give thanks to him in song."

Psalm 84:12 "O Lord Almighty, blessed is the man who trusts in you."

Proverbs 118:8 "It is better to take refuge in the Lord than to trust in man."

Proverbs 3:5 "Trust in the Lord with all your heart and lean not to your own understanding."

Proverbs 11:28 "Whoever trusts in his riches will fall, but the righteous will thrive like a green leaf."

Proverbs 31:10-11 "Who can find a virtuous wife? For her worth is far above rubies. The heart of her husband safely trusts her; so he will have no lack of gain."

Quotes:

"Love all, trust a few, do wrong to none." Shakespeare

"Trust is like an eraser, it gets smaller and smaller after every mistake." Unknown

"Trust takes years to build, seconds to break, and forever to repair." Unknown

There are many verses that tell us we should put our trust in God. The Bible tells us that men will fail us, governments will fail us, and riches will fail us. We shouldn't even count on our own instincts or thoughts without God's direction (Proverbs 3:5). I did find it interesting that the one place it talks about trusting someone was a husband/wife relationship (Proverbs 31:11).

Today I pray that you trust in the Lord. Trust in Him brings protection, provision, and peace. When you understand that He directs your paths, it's easy to recognize His leading when it comes. I pray that God puts trustworthy people around you and that I will always be the wife that you need and on whom you can depend. I also ask that you continue to be a person that others know is full of honesty, integrity, and reliability.

Day 23

HUMILITY

James 4:6 "But He gives more grace. Therefore it says, 'God opposes the proud, but gives grace to the humble.'"

Philippians 2:3 "Do nothing from rivalry or conceit, but in humility count others more significant than yourselves."

Proverbs 22:4 "The reward for humility and fear of the Lord is riches and honor and life."

James 4:10 "Humble yourselves before the Lord, and He will exalt you."

Proverbs 11:2 "When pride comes, then comes disgrace, but with the humble is wisdom."

Psalm 25:9 "He leads the humble in what is right, and teaches the humble His way."

Psalm 138:6 "For though the Lord is high, He regards the lowly, but the haughty He knows from afar."

Proverbs 3:34 "Toward the scorners, He is scornful, but to the humble He gives favor."

Quotes:

"There is nothing noble in being superior to your fellow man; true nobility is being superior to your former self." Ernest Hemingway

"True humility is not thinking less of yourself; it is thinking of yourself less." C.S. Lewis

"These are the few ways we can practice humility:
To speak as little as possible of one's self.
To mind one's own business.
Not to want to manage other people's affairs.
To avoid curiosity.
To accept contradictions and correction cheerfully.
To pass over the mistakes of others.
To accept insult and injuries.
To accept being slighted, forgotten, and disliked.
To be kind and gentle even under provocation.
Never to stand on one's dignity.
To choose always the hardest." Mother Teresa

In Luke 18:9-14, Jesus is telling a parable to a bunch of church folks. He says, two men went to the temple, one a Pharisee and the other a tax collector. The Pharisee prays "with himself" (verse 11). He wasn't being loud so everyone around him could hear; he was praying quietly to himself. "God thank you that I'm not caught up in sin like a lot of other people. You know I fast twice a week and I tithe off of everything I have, I'm doing what you commanded of me." The tax collector, on the other hand, stood in the corner with his head bowed, beat his chest, and said, "God, be merciful to me, a sinner!" The exclamation point at the end of the sentence makes me think that he wasn't being so quiet. I'm sure he was getting attention from everyone in the temple, since the Pharisee even begins to mention him in his prayer (verse 11). But Jesus said the tax collector was the one who left justified. The Pharisee's sin wasn't in his bragging to the other church folks about how righteous he was … it was a heart thing. He was so caught up in pride that he sincerely believed that he was better than everyone else around him. He was doing good things (fasting, praying, tithing), but he began to believe that doing good things somehow made him good. He obviously forgot the scripture in Isaiah 64:6, "All of us have become like one who is unclean; and all our righteous acts are like filthy rags; we all shrivel up like a leaf, and like the wind our sins sweep us away." Jesus was trying to teach a very strong lesson on humility. One of the quickest ways to catch the eyes of God is to have a humble spirit.

Today I pray that you always possess a humble heart. I ask that your actions this week will reveal that you are a man who reacts with kindness and humility. I pray that God blesses your meekness, like His word says, with wisdom, grace, riches, honor, and life. I also ask that He allows you to reap kindness and humility from others when difficult situations arise.

Day 24
THANKFULNESS

1 Thessalonians 5:18 “Give thanks in all circumstances; for this is the will of God in Christ Jesus for you.”

Psalm 106:1 “Praise the Lord! Oh give thanks to the Lord, for he is good, for his steadfast love endures forever!”

James 1:7 “Every good gift and every perfect gift is from above, coming down from the Father of lights with whom there is no variation or shadow due to change.”

1 Chronicles 16:8 “Oh give thanks to the Lord; call upon his name; make known his deeds among the people!”

Psalm 116:12 “What shall I render to the Lord for all his benefits to me?”

Romans 1:21 “For although they knew God, they did not honor him as God or give thanks to him, but they became futile in their thinking and their foolish hearts were darkened.”

Quotes:

“The Pilgrims made seven times more graves than huts. No Americans have been more impoverished than these who, nevertheless, set aside a day of thanksgiving.” H.U. Westermayer

"God gave you a gift of 86,400 seconds today. Have you used one to say, 'Thank you'?" William Arthur Ward

"The hardest arithmetic to master is that which enables us to count our blessings." Eric Hoffer

"Feeling gratitude and not expressing it is like wrapping a present and not giving it." William Arthur Ward

"Gratitude is the sign of a noble soul." Aesop

Today I pray that you stop and take notice of all the blessings that surround you. I like what Psalm 116:12 says, "What shall I render to the Lord for all his benefits to me?" The answer is … thankfulness. He only asks that we acknowledge His goodness; recognize that He is the one who blesses our lives daily. Simple? Yes. Do we do it regularly? No. In Luke 17:11-19, we read the story of the ten lepers. Jesus heals them all, but only one comes back to show his gratitude. It almost seems like Jesus is surprised by this. He says, "'Were there not ten cleansed? Where are the nine? Were there not any found who returned to give glory to God except this foreigner?' And He said to him, 'Arise, go your way. Your faith has made you well.'" Jesus acquainted being thankful with faith. If we truly have faith in Christ, then we will find ourselves thanking Him daily for the goodness He showers on us. I pray that you recognize all the good gifts in your life and take a moment today to thank God for them.

Day 25
REST

Psalm 127:2 "It is in vain that you rise up early and go late to rest, eating the bread of anxious toil; for he gives to his beloved sleep."

Mark 6:31 "And he said to them, 'Come away by yourselves to a desolate place and rest awhile.' For many were coming and going, and they had no leisure even to eat."

Proverbs 3:24 "If you lie down, you will not be afraid; when you lie down, your sleep will be sweet."

Exodus 33:14 "And he said, 'My presence shall go with you, and I will give you rest.'"

Hebrews 4:9-10 "There remaineth therefore a rest to the people of God. For he that is entered into his rest, he also has ceased from his own works, as God did from his."

Psalm 16:9 "Therefore my heart is glad and my tongue rejoices; my body also will rest secure."

Job 11:18 "You will live secure and full of hope; God will protect you and give you rest."

Quotes:

"He that can take rest is greater than he that can take cities." Benjamin Franklin

"I still need more healthy rest in order to work at my best. My health is the main capital I have and I want to administer it intelligently." Ernest Hemingway

"Every now and then go away, have a little relaxation, for when you come back to your work, your judgment will be surer." Leonardo da Vinci

"The life of inner peace, being harmonious and without stress, is the easiest type of existence." Norman Vincent Peale

Today I pray for you to be able to rest. I ask that your mind and body will quickly find the sleep that you need in order to accomplish the goals that you have set for yourself. God designed us in a way that one-third of our day should be spent sleeping. In Genesis 2:1-3, we read where God rested on the seventh day from all His work. Then He blessed and sanctified that day. Why did God need to rest in the first place? Psalm 121:4 says, "Behold, He who keeps Israel shall neither slumber nor sleep." God didn't take a day off from all His creating because He needed a break; He was setting an example for us. God expects you to work hard, but He also expects you to balance that work with some downtime. The Sabbath is a day to redirect our attention from trying to provide for ourselves and our families to focusing on the One who gives us the ability to work in the first place. Our bodies need rest to be healthy and regenerate itself; our minds need quiet time to find peace and tranquility, and our souls need time to commune with our Creator to find our life's purpose. I pray that tonight you have the best night's sleep that you've had in a long time.

Day 26
PURPOSE

John 15:16 "You did not choose me, but I chose you and appointed you that you should go and bear fruit and that your fruit should abide, so that whatever you ask the Father in my name, he may give it to you."

Jeremiah 29:11 "For I know the plans I have for you, declares the Lord, plans of peace and not of evil, to give you a future and a hope."

Ecclesiastes 12:13 "The end of the matter; all has been heard. Fear God and keep his commandments, for this is the whole duty of man."

1 Thessalonians 4:11 "And to aspire to live quietly, and to mind your own affairs, and to work with your hands, as we commanded you."

Philippians 1:6 "And I am sure of this, that he who began a good work in you will bring it to completion at the day of Jesus Christ."

Quotes:

"The two most important days of your life are the day you are born and the day you find out why." Mark Twain

"The only thing that stands between a man and what he wants from life is often merely the will to try it and the faith to believe that it is possible." David Viscott

"The meaning of life is to find your gift. The purpose of life is to give it away." Pablo Picasso

"Ships in harbors are safe, but that's not what ships are built for." John Shedd

Everyone is looking to discover what our purpose in life is. There are numerous books written on the subject. The Bible is very direct and simplistic about what our purpose on this earth is … we are here to glorify God, keep His commandments, and point others to Him. The confusion comes in when we try to figure out just how to do those things. The answer is not the same for everyone. If it were, we could look to each other to find our own destiny. In Matthew 25:14-30, we find the parable of the talents. The lord of the house handed out different amounts of talents to his servants, one received five, one received two and the last received one. The first two went out and doubled their talents, but the last one just hid his. The lord of the house blessed the first two servants, but chastised the last servant calling him wicked and lazy. God gives each one of us different talents (abilities, interests, gifts, skills, etc.). It's what we decide to do with them that count! If we use our talents for Christ, we find our purpose in life. The things we do well (talents) begin to grow and compound. We get joy and satisfaction out of doing the very things that God created in us. The flip side of the coin is if we are jealous of others' gifts, feel ours is insignificant or don't use them for the right reasons, we will never reach our full potential. The wicked and lazy servant made a choice … he hid the *Lord's talent* (verse 25 "I was afraid and went and ***hid thy talent*** in the earth"). It belonged to God to start with, He just allowed the servant to use it to see what he would accomplish with it. Unfortunately, he could not see how his talent was connected to his destiny and purpose. His life was unfulfilled, fearful, and discontented. In the end, the Lord took his one talent and gave it to the servant who had ten. Our purpose in this life is to take our gifts and find ways to magnify Christ with them. Never discount the things that come easy to you; if you can sing … sing, if you can teach … teach, if you can write … write. You get the picture. Just because certain things, aka gifts, come naturally to you—don't assume that they come easily to others. Those very things are your God-given talents … invest them wisely!

Today I pray that your purpose is always evident to you. God has gifted you in many areas. I ask Him to multiply your talents as you use them to further His kingdom. I pray that you find joy and satisfaction in doing the things that come "naturally" to you and that you reach your full potential in this life.

Day 27
PERFECT HEART

Deuteronomy 18:13 "Thou shalt be perfect with the Lord thy God."

Psalm 37:37 "Mark the perfect man and behold the upright; for the end of that man is peace."

1 Kings 8:61 "Let your heart therefore be perfect with the Lord our God, to walk in his statues and to keep his commandments as at this day."

<u>Men that God called perfect</u>:

Noah-Genesis 6:9 "Noah was a just man and perfect in his generation, and Noah walked with God."

Job-Job 1:8 "And the Lord said unto Satan, Hast thou considered my servant Job, that there is none like him in the earth, a perfect and upright man, one that fears God and turns away from evil?"

David-1 Kings 11:4 "And it came to pass when Solomon was old, that his wives turned away his heart after other gods: and his heart was not perfect with the Lord his God, as was the heart of David his father."

Asa-1 Kings 15:14 "Nevertheless Asa's heart was perfect with the Lord all his days."

Quotes:

"Strive for perfection in everything you do. Take the best that exists and make it better. When it does not exist, design it." Sir Henry Royce

"It is only imperfection that complains of what is imperfect. The more perfect we are, the more gentle and quiet we become towards the defects of others." Joseph Addison

Today I pray that you have a perfect heart in the eyes of God. We know that the word "perfect" in these scriptures can't mean sinless. Each of the above men had their sin(s) documented in the Word of God. Noah got naked and drunk in front of his family, Job questioned why God would allow bad to come into his life, Asa put his confidence in a king and physicians instead of God, and David was a murderer and adulterer. In the original Greek and Hebrew, the word "perfect" means complete, finished, wholehearted or full grown. These men did not live blameless lives, but they were entirely committed to their God. They found completeness in their relationship with Him and recognized who He was. They didn't live sinless, but they also never doubted God's existence, abilities, and provision. They were perfect or whole because they depended on Him to fill in the holes and deficiencies in their lives. They knew their weaknesses could only be overcome with the help from God. Ecclesiastes 7:20 says, "For there is not a just man upon earth that doeth good and sinneth not." We cannot live a completely sinless life, but we can strive for excellence in living Christlike. We can have a perfect heart by never doubting who God is and the impact He has on our lives. All of these men had a relationship with God and sought His direction for their lives. My prayer is that you live in such a way that God views you as perfect in His eyes.

Day 28
FORGIVENESS

Ephesians 4:32 "Be kind to one another, tenderhearted, forgiving one another, as God in Christ forgave you."

Proverbs 25:21-22 "If your enemy is hungry, give him bread to eat, and if he is thirsty, give him water to drink, for you will heap burning coals on his head, and the Lord will reward you."

Matthew 5:44 "But I say to you, love your enemies and pray for those who persecute you."

Luke 17:3-4 "Pay attention to yourselves! If your brother sins, rebuke him, and if he repents, forgive him and if he sins against you seven times in a day, and turns to you seven times, saying, 'I repent,' you must forgive him."

Quotes:

"Apologizing does not always mean you are wrong and the other person is right. It just means you value your relationship more than your ego." Unknown

"Genuine forgiveness does not deny anger, but faces it head on." Alice Duer Miller

"You will achieve more in this world through acts of mercy than you will through acts of retribution." Nelson Mandela

"Forgiveness is a funny thing. It warms the heart and cools the sting." William Arthur Ward

Today I pray that you always have a forgiving spirit. This may be the toughest devotion yet. I read a quote that said our forgiveness is matched to our love. While it is not easy, we seem to be able to forgive those closest to us. We can excuse their behavior and justify why we need to repair the relationship, but the Bible doesn't just tell us to forgive our family, friends or coworkers for wronging us. It specifically says our enemies, those who set out with intentional harm in mind … forgive them, too? YES! Remember these verses, "Do not repay evil with evil or insult with insult. On the contrary, repay evil with blessing, because to this you were called so that you may inherit a blessing" (1 Peter 3:9). Or what about, "Bless those who curse you, pray for those who mistreat you" (Luke 6:28). God requires that we forgive everyone, every time, without reservation. This could be one of the most difficult requirements of a Christlike life. This is one lesson that takes true discipline to accomplish. I pray that you find the inner strength to see past any wrong done to you and are able to make the choice to forgive those who did it!

Day 29

SEXUAL PURITY

1 Corinthians 6:18 “Flee from sexual immorality. Every other sin a person commits is outside the body, but the sexually immoral person sins against his own body.”

Colossians 3:5 “Put to death therefore what is earthly in you: sexual immorality, impurity, passion, evil desire, and covetousness which is idolatry.”

Psalm 119:133 “Keep steady my steps according to your promise, and let no iniquity get dominion over me.”

2 Corinthians 7:1 “Since we have these promises, beloved, let us cleanse ourselves from every defilement of body and spirit, bringing holiness to completion in the fear of God.”

2 Timothy 2:22 “So flee youthful passions and pursue righteousness, faith, love and peace, along with those who call on the Lord from a pure heart.”

Romans 12:2 “Do not be conformed to this world, but be transformed by the renewal of your mind, that by testing you may discern what is the will of God, what is good and acceptable and perfect.”

Quotes:

“Either sin will keep you from the Word or the Word will keep you from sin.” John Bunyun

"Our strength is visible in what we stand for, and our weakness in what makes us fall." Vivian Griffis

"Love does not consist in gazing at each other, but in looking together in the same direction." Antoine de Saint

Since the beginning of time, man has battled with sexual sins. The Bible gives quite a list of people who fell into this temptation: David (adultery), Shechem (rape), Amnon (incest), Solomon (polygamy), and Judah (slept with his daughter-in-law thinking she was a prostitute). Each of these men found out the hard way that the cost for these sins was high.

Unfortunately, we have to deal with things today that earlier generations did not. We live in a technological age where sex sells, so it is everywhere we look and listen. You turn on the TV and there it is right in front of you, you open a benign magazine and there is an advertisement, you drive down the interstate and pass an explicit billboard, you go online and for goodness sakes, don't misspell a word because you don't know what is going to pop up, or you can just flip through the radio stations to hear all sorts of vulgar song lyrics.

Exodus 20:14 says, "You shall not commit adultery." Then in Matthew 5:28 Jesus himself declares, "Whosoever looks on a woman to lust after her has already committed adultery with her in his heart." So … he went from the very act is a sin, to just contemplating it is. God takes our sexual purity very seriously and warns us of the destruction that comes from not guarding it (1 Thessalonians 4:3-8 … "because the Lord is the avenger of all such, as we also forewarned you and testified"). If we think we can fight this temptation alone, especially these days, we are fooling ourselves. God's grace is our only hope. Not just to forgive us when we do sin, but to give us the strength to resist the temptation in the first place.

Today I pray that you are pure in heart, mind, and body. I ask that when you are tempted to yield that God supplies you with the ability and grace to say, "No." I pray that He also gives you the wisdom and strength to stay away from situations that would lead you down the wrong road. You are a man who will live soberly, righteously, and godly in this present age (Titus 2:11-12 NIV)!

Day 30

FAITH

Hebrews 11:6 "And without faith it is impossible to please him, for whoever would draw near to God must believe that he exists and that he rewards those who seek him."

Romans 10:7 "So faith comes from hearing, and hearing through the word of Christ."

Hebrews 11:1 "Faith is the substance of things hoped for, the evidence not seen."

2 Corinthians 5:7 "For we walk by faith, not by sight."

James 2:18 "But someone will say, 'You have faith and I have works.' Show me your faith apart from your works, and I will show you my faith by my works."

Matthew 17:20 "He replied, 'because you have so little faith. I tell you the truth, if you have faith as small as a mustard seed, you can say to this mountain, move from here to there and it will move. Nothing will be impossible for you.'"

Quotes:

"I have been driven many times upon my knees by the overwhelming conviction that I had nowhere else to go. My own wisdom and that of all about me seemed insufficient for that day." Abraham Lincoln

"To one who has faith, no explanation is necessary, to one without faith, no explanation is possible." St Thomas Aquinas

"Faith is seeing light with your heart, when all your eyes see is darkness." Unknown

"Faith is the art of holding on to things in spite of your changing moods and circumstances." C.S. Lewis

One of the best examples of faith in action is in Matthew 15:21-28. A Canaanite woman comes to Jesus crying and begging Him to heal her demon-possessed daughter. Jesus' reaction seems strange; He doesn't even acknowledge her. The disciples finally ask Jesus to send her away because she keeps bothering them. The woman comes and worships Christ and says, "Lord, help me!" He tells her that it's not good to take the children's bread and give it to dogs. But her response catches Jesus' attention, "Yes, Lord, yet even the little dogs eat the crumbs which fall from their masters' table." She had seen and heard enough about Jesus to know that He was the source of help that her daughter so desperately needed. Faith is the substance of things hoped for, the evidence not seen. Nothing in this story prior to this moment led that woman to believe that Christ was going to help her … the fact was He was ignoring her! But there was something inside her that drove her to continue on. She was like Peter, in John 6:68, "Lord, to whom shall we go? Thou hast the words of eternal life. And we believe and are sure that thou art that Christ, the Son of the living God." All she had was the hope that Jesus would move in her situation, even though the situation looked hopeless. That "something inside her," (her faith) caused Jesus to stop what He was doing, neglect the crowds that were around Him and speak directly to her. "O woman, great is your faith! Let it be to you as you desire," and her daughter was immediately healed. Our faith grabs God's attention and causes Him to move on our behalf!

Today I pray that your faith is increased. As a father, it would bother you to find out that one of our children desperately needed something and chose to ask somebody else to give it to them. Especially, if you had exactly what it was that they needed. You would wonder what had breached your relationship that made them feel that they could no longer depend on you. I believe our God is like that….

He has everything we could ever need (healing, peace, finances, joy, solutions, you fill in the blank), but we often look elsewhere for the answers. It's like we are saying, "I don't trust you God with this." Faith is more than just believing that God exists; it believes that He is able and willing to handle every situation that I bring to Him! I pray that you have the kind of persistent faith that makes God take notice.

Day 31

DRESS FOR SUCCESS

Isaiah 11:5 "Righteousness shall be the belt of his waist, and faithfulness the belt of his loins."

Ephesians 6:11-17 "Put on the whole armor of God that you may be able to stand against the schemes of the devil. For we do not wrestle against flesh and blood, but against the rulers, against the authorities, against the cosmic powers over this present darkness, against the spiritual forces of evil in the heavenly places. Therefore take up the whole armor of God that you may be able to withstand in the evil day, and having done all, to stand firm. Stand therefore, having fastened on the belt of truth, and having put on the breastplate of righteousness, and as shoes for your feet, having put on the readiness given by the gospel of peace. In all circumstances take up the shield of faith, with which you can extinguish all the flaming darts of the evil one; and take the helmet of salvation, and the sword of the Spirit, which is the Word of God."

Quotes:

"Opportunity is missed by most people because it is dressed in overalls and looks like work." Thomas Edison

"God has amazing plans for your life. The enemy, too, has plans for you. So be ready for both and be wise enough to know which one to battle and which one to embrace." Unknown

"A grandfather told his young grandson, 'My son, there is a battle between two wolves inside all of us. One is evil. It is anger, jealousy, greed, resentment, inferiority, lies, and ego. The other is good. It is joy, peace, love, hope, humility, kindness, compassion, and truth.' The little boy thought about it and asked, 'Grandpa, which wolf wins?' The old man quietly replied, 'The one you feed.'" Unknown

We are taught that we should dress for the job we want and the impression we desire to make. Our outer appearance often reflects who we are on the inside and people quickly make an assessment about us by our clothing choices. Today, I pray that you dress for success. However, I'm not talking about picking out a nicely starched shirt, colorful tie, or your favorite pair of dress pants. I'm asking God to help you be successful in whatever comes your way today. The Bible tells us that we should daily dress ourselves with His armor, so that we are not vulnerable to the devil's tactics. 1 Peter 5:8 says that Satan is roaming around seeking people to tear up or devour, and those without protection become easy prey! I pray that your mind is protected from any doubts or worry (helmet of salvation), that your heart is guarded (breastplate of righteousness), your words are true and trustworthy (belt of truth), that your feet are swift to spread peace everywhere you go (gospel of peace) and, lastly, that your faith is a defense against evil (shield of faith/sword of the Spirit). Today you will succeed!!

EPILOGUE

My prayer is that this devotion book has somehow enriched and strengthened your relationship with your spouse. I hope that as you have given yourself to some personal study and prayer time, you, too, have grown in the areas that you have so earnestly prayed for your husband. Mark 11:24 says, "Therefore I tell you, whatever you ask in prayer, believe that you have received it, and it will be yours." Remember that life can sometimes become overwhelming and chaotic. It is so easy to get caught up in trying to just keep up. As a woman, you are often expected to wear many hats: wife, mother, cook, teacher, chauffeur, maid, volunteer, boo-boo kisser, sideline cheerleader, businesswoman, and on and on and on.... Never forget that in the midst of this journey that we call life, one of your greatest accomplishments is being a wife who supports her husband in prayer. Guard yourself against overcommitment. A strong marriage creates the very foundation of a loving, productive family. Never underestimate the power that you possess as a praying woman! Make a conscious decision to be proactive in your prayers regarding your husband. Realize your role and importance in the success of your marriage. My personal prayer for you today is "The Lord bless you and keep you; the Lord make his face to shine upon you and be gracious to you; the Lord lift up his countenance upon you and give you peace" (Numbers 6:24-26). May God always richly bless you and your family!

CPSIA information can be obtained
at www.ICGtesting.com
Printed in the USA
LVHW011503180821
695285LV00002B/2